Also,

By Barbara Williams Brown

*Shadows of the Pheonix*

Finding Purpose and The Revelation of Beauty in The Face of Pain

*Finding Purpose and The Revelation of Beauty  
In The Face of Pain*

BARBARA WILLIAMS BROWN

Finding Purpose and The Revelation of Beauty in The Face of Pain

**NOTE:** The sale of this book without its cover is unauthorized. If you purchased this book without a cover, you should be aware that it was reported to the publisher as "unsold and destroyed." Neither the author nor the publisher has received payments for the sale of this stripped book.

The quotes and ideas in this book, other than scripture verses, are not accurate in all cases. Some of them have been edited for clarity and brevity. In all cases, the author has attempted to maintain the original intent of the characters.

Names have been changed and are either products of the author's imagination, personal experiences of some of the coessential characters, or are used fictitiously. Any resemblance to actual events or locales or person, living or dead is entirely coincidental.

No portion of this book may be reproduced, stored in a retrieval system, or transmitted in any form by any means-electronic, mechanical, photocopy, recording, or other-except for brief quotations in printed reviews, without prior permission of the author.

DBEM Publishing
133 Annacy Park Drive
Columbia, SC 29223

Finding Purpose and The Revelation of Beauty in The Face of Pain

Copyright 2024 by BARBARA WILLIAMS BROWN

All rights reserved

Cover art by Deryl Brown

ISBN: 978-1-7358061-4-3

Printed in the United States

First Edition

## Dedication

*This book is dedicated to people everywhere experiencing some type of pain. Though it is not a solution, it is designed to be both inspirational and motivational. I dedicate this book in the loving memory of my dear mother, Emmie Singletary Williams Dozier. She has been the foundation for all my successes, with her words of wisdom and her pool of knowledge. I would also like to dedicate this book to my children, Deryl and Tiffany and to my four grandsons, Demarrias, Breyan, Eli 'sha, and Tai Tenn. These are the ones that keep me encouraged as I struggle through this beautiful and sometimes painful life. Lastly, but in no way the least, I would like to dedicate this book to my sister Emmie J. Davis who often comes by or calls to see how I am doing and encourages me by example. And to all of you that have taken the time to read my book, I dedicate it to you.*

Finding Purpose and The Revelation of Beauty in The Face of Pain

# Acknowledgements

I would like to acknowledge and thank my heavenly father for the gift of writing, and for sustainability. I would like to thank my son Deryl for my amazing book cover and design, and all his help in publishing this book.

Finding Purpose and The Revelation of Beauty in The Face of Pain

Grace Hill is a righteous woman, the mother of one daughter, Jackie, and the grandmother of two children, Zelia and Damon. She's a strong woman that always have a positive outlook, even during the middle of a raging storm. When face with a dilemma, Grace always sees the glass as half filled as opposed to being half empty. She taught her daughter to be fearless, and to always go after her dreams without second guessing herself. When her husband was tragically killed in an automobile accident, people expected her to fall apart, because she and her husband Tard had been together since grade school and were very close. They were married two weeks after they graduated high school and went off to the same college. After graduation, the couple got jobs and began saving up for their first home. They lived in a one-bedroom apartment with one bathroom and a small kitchen and family room, but they were as happy as two people could be.

One morning after they had been living in the apartment for around five years, Grace did not get out of bed to prepare for work as she usually did. Tard had taken his shower and headed for the kitchen as he had done for years. Usually, Grace would follow because he always made breakfast for the two of them. When he'd finished making breakfast and setting it on the table, he sat to wait for Grace. After five minutes of waiting, he called out to her; "hey, your gunner be late, what's up with you this morning?" When he didn't get a reply, he became concerned, and rushed to the bedroom to see if anything was wrong. He found Grace still in bed wrapped in a blanket. "Grace, are you ok, what's wrong honey?" "Tard, I feel awful, I'm not going to make it to work today, I can't move." "You don't expect me to leave you in this condition, do you?" Tard got on the phone and called his office. Since he was the owner and CEO of his company, he could call the shots. He explained to Candace, his secretary, that he would probably not be in the office at all today and had her rescheduled any appointments he had scheduled. "Okay Mr. Hill, will Mrs. Hill be coming in today?" Grace was senior vice president of affairs at her husband's company. "No, Candance, neither of us will be in today, thank you."

When Tard hung up the phone, he walked over to the bed where his wife was still curled up in a ball, and asked, "so, what are we having a boy or a girl?" Normally Grace was hard to rouse, but she looked at Tard as if he had just made an appearance from Mars. "What on earth are you talking about? I am about to puke my inside out, and you're asking me some silly question, I think that I need to see a doctor, Tard, I don't feel well at all, and I think I have a fever." Tard obediently picked up the phone again to call the doctor, but not before pulling his wife into his arms to comfort her. She rested her head on his shoulder as he dialed the number. He explained Grace's symptoms to the doctor, and no, she didn't have a fever. When he hung up from the doctor, Grace asked; so, what did the doctor say, can he see us today?" "Yes, he will see you in an hour if you can make that time." "I will just have to; I feel as if I'm dying." "You are not dying honey even though you may feel like it." "What about breakfast?" "What about it?" "Do you want any?" "No, I do not want any breakfast, the thought of it is making me worse." "Okay dear, no breakfast." Tard was a calm and quiet man and had the patience of Job.

Grace went into the bathroom to take a quick shower and was out in under thirty minutes. "That was fast, what did you do, run through the water?" Despite her bad feelings, Grace had to laugh. "Tard." "Yes honey." "What made you ask me if we are having a boy or girl, are you ready to start a family?" "Ready or not here we come."

"Come on Tard, be serious. Suppose we are pregnant; how would you feel about it?" "As long as you are healthy, I would be on top of the moon with excitement." "Well, let's table this discussion until later when I'm feeling much better." "Okay, we will for now, but we will probably pick it back up once we leave the doctor's office." "Whatever Tard."

Just as Tard predicted, after the doctor had finished examining Grace, he came out smiling. "Well Grace and Tard, you are going to be parents." Tard jumped up out of his chair and made a whopping sound. Grace just sat there with her mouth gapped open. After the initial shock, Grace began to cry. "What's wrong honey, why are you crying?" "I never said anything to you, but I was beginning to think that I was never going to get pregnant." "Why would you think that?" I don't know, probable because we were married almost five years, and nothing happened." "It just wasn't our time honey, but now it is, and I can't wait to tell my parents." "Yeah, they have been bugging us for a while now about grandkids." "Can we not tell them just yet though; I want to make sure everything is good and that the baby and me are healthy." "Sure, whenever you are ready, not a minute before." Both Grace and Tard were besides themselves with joy; everywhere they went for the next several weeks, they had these fixed smiles on their faces as if they knew something that the rest of the world did not.

When Grace went in for her three-month checkup, the doctor informed her that everything looked well and that she and the baby were both healthy. Up until this appointment, Tard had always accompanied her, but he had an important meeting to attend that he just couldn't get out off, and Grace had told him that she would be alright going alone. She left the doctor's office happy and couldn't wait to get to Tard to tell him the good news. When she arrived at his office, he was still in his meeting, so she waited as if she was a client. When his meeting finally ended, Candace looked over at her and said, "Mrs. Hill, Mr. Hill can see you now." "Thank you, Candace." When she reached Tard's office, she tapped on the door. "Yes, come in." Grace opened the door and poked her head in. Mr. Hill looked up to see who was entering and burst into laughter when he saw it was his wife. "Well hello mam, please come in and have a seat." "Thank you, kind sir, but I am too excited to sit." "Tell me, did you find out the gender?" "No not today, I asked if they would reschedule it until you are able to be there with me." "Great, so how did the appointment go?" "It went really, well. The doctor said that both the baby and me are healthy and doing well." "Well, that's a relief. So, can we tell somebody now?" "Yes, we can; we will have a dinner party and invite your parents, then give them the good news." "When?" "Tonight, I am leaving now to prepare." "Don't overdo it Grace, do you need me to help?" "Can you get away?" Tard looked at his watch, and then his calendar, and said, yes, let's do this." Grace and Tard rushed out of his office to go and prepare for the dinner party with his parents. "So, Tard, are we inviting anyone else tonight beside your parents?" "Do you want to invite someone else?" "Not really, not since it's such short notice, but I wanted to know if we were on the same page." "We are, as always." "Okay then, just you, me, and your mom and dad."

The dinner party with Tard's parents went well. They were so excited that they were getting a grandbaby. "Tell me, asked Tard senior, what are we having?" "We are not having anything," laughed Nancy, his mom. Everyone laughed at Nancy's remark. "Seriously though, asked Nancy, do you know if it's a boy or girl?" "No, we don't, responded Grace, we will find out at the next appointment." After the news was broken and Tard's parents had gone home, he looked over at his wife and asked, "are you going to tell your parents Grace?" "Yes, I guess I will have too at some point, I am just not in a hurry to do so." Grace's parents never wanted her to marry Tard. They thought that she had married beneath her, and because of it, they never visited or called. The only communication came from Grace. She called her parents every Sunday evening despite their cold dispositions. "Whenever I tell them it will be over the phone. If they say something negative that I don't want to hear, I will just hang up." "No Grace, we are going to Florida, and tell them in person. I am no longer a timid boy, but a man, and soon to be father. This nonsense needs to end now; I should have ended it a long time ago." Grace was impressed with her husband for taking authority. "So, when do you suggest we go to Florida, Tard?" "I am going to book us a flight, and I don't intend to tell them that we are coming, I am just going to show up on their doorsteps and come what may." "Do you think that's a good idea?" "No, but it's the only one I have at the moment."

Just as Tard suggested, he booked a flight to Florida for the two of them. Neither told her parents that they would be coming. Grace was somewhat nervous, but Tard was pumped. He wanted to put an end to the gap between Grace and her parents. He didn't care if they accepted him or disapproved of him. He had parents, he wasn't looking for anymore. "Are you nervous Tard?" "About what?" "Meeting my parents?" "No, I'm not; they should be ashamed of themselves; they didn't have the decency to show up at their only daughter's wedding for some pettiness and continues to hold on to their stupid prides. They have missed out on a lot of your life's milestones, but I refuse to let them miss out on our child, or children." "Thanks, Tard." "For what baby?" "For doing this, it should have been dealt with a long time ago, but I just got fed up with them downing you every time we spoke." "No thanks needed honey, after today, they are either in or out, not in between."

The following Friday, both Grace and Tard took of work to make the trip to Florida. They had decided to go on Friday and make it a long weekend. After a short discussion, they both decided that staying at a hotel would be the best choice. Since they were not giving her parents any advance notice of their arrival, they didn't want to end up with the surprise being on them. It had been quite some time since Grace had visited her parents. She refused to go alone when she had a husband, simply because they didn't approve of him. They had an early flight that required them to be at the airport by seven AM. Although Grace was a little apprehensive about the trip, she was also excited. Not just because she would see her parents again, but because she had such great news to share with them. She was an only child, so she was their only source for grandchildren. Grace was born Grace Elizabeth

Henderson. Her parents Diane and Bradley Henderson often referred to her as being their sole heir. Both her parents were only children. Mr. and Mrs. Henderson had done well for themselves. They were both successful in their careers and were quite wealthy. As a child, Grace was always pampered, and treated like royalty. She never allowed her head to swell because of her parents' riches.

After Grace and Tard boarded the plane, and were getting ready for takeoff, she looked over at Tard with a devastated expression on her face. "What is it honey, having second thoughts?" "You know I sort of am, I know this is the right thing to do, but frankly, I'm not in the mood for another round with my parents about you." "Don't worry baby, I can handle myself, besides, I will not allow them to upset you. As I said earlier, they are either all the way in or all the way out, there's no compromise." Grace smiled at her husband as her heart filled with admiration. Not everyone got to be so blessed with a husband such as hers, especially at a young age. She leaned her head on his broad shoulder with pride and confidence, knowing that he would make things right. "Tard." "Yes." "Why have you decided that now is the time to make peace? Why haven't you attempted before?" "Because the timing must be right. Everything has a purpose and a season; if I had attempted earlier, things may have gotten out of hand. Now that we have all matured, not only in our characteristics, but also in our spirituality, our patience and tolerance should have grown. As Christians, we should be able to put petti differences aside for the sake of our salvation." "Wow! Well said."

The plane ride from Atlanta Georgia to Palm Beach Florida was very pleasant and took a few minutes under an hour. When Grace exited the plane, she exhaled; "so close, but yet, so far away." Tard did not have an outward response for her, but he thought to himself, "not after today." After they had settled in their hotel room, they decided to go out and get some breakfast before starting their quest. "So, what would you like to eat?" asked Tard. Grace could not make up her mind, so Tard chose for her. They'd found a cozy little breakfast café and decided that it was the perfect place to have breakfast. Tard ordered shrimp and grits, something they had not eaten in a long while, but both loved. Instead of coffee, he ordered hibiscus tea for Grace. He also added toast and fruit. Grace had quite an appetite after she'd gotten over her morning sickness. Grace downed her meal as if she had not eaten in days.

"My that was good. I am glad you picked the restaurant and the meal; I could not decide on anything." "Why was that?" Because I wanted everything," she laughed. Grace and Tard left the restaurant holding hands and headed back to the hotel. Before leaving Atlanta, Tard had arranged for a rental car to be delivered to the hotel. When they arrived, the car had been delivered and the keys were left at the front desk as instructed. "Ok Mrs. Hill, shall we begin our pursuit?" "Sure, but I need to go up to the room and refresh, I have a feeling this is going to be a long sweaty day."

Without an invitation, Grace and Tard headed for her parent's home. Grace felt a little shaky, but Tard was as cool as a cucumber. He could feel Graces's uneasiness, so he began singing to her.

"When the night has come
And the land is dark
And the moon is the only light
we'll see
No, I won't be afraid
Oh, I won't be afraid
Just as long as you stand, stand by me
So darlin', darlin', stand by me
Oh, stand by me
Oh, stand
Stand by me, stand by me."
If the sky that we look upon
Should tumble and fall

Or the mountain should crumble to
the sea
I won't cry, I won't cry
No, I won't shed a tear
Just as long as you stand
Stand by me
And darlin', darlin', stand by me
Oh, stand by me
Oh, stand now
Stand by me, stand by me."

"You sure know how to put a girl's mind at ease." "I try madam, I try." Grace was so caught up in Tard's singing, that she didn't realize that they were pulling up in her parents' driveway. "Why are we stopping?" "Because we have arrived." She looked up and gasped. "Calm down honey, they are only your parents, not some type of monsters." "Touche'."

Tard got out of the car and went around to the passenger side to let Grace out. He caught her by the hand as she pulled herself up from the seat. Once out of the car, he placed his arms around her waist, and began walking towards the front entrance of her parents' home. "Do you think they're home?" asked Grace. "Of course, they are, it's midday Friday, where else would they be?" "I guess you're right, they both work from home now, so unless they are playing hooky, they should be inside." When they reached the door, Tard leaned in and rang the doorbell. Without bothering to ask who it was, Mrs. Henderson flung the door open as if she was expecting someone. When she saw Grace and Tard standing there, she was stunned. "Hello" she said in a wobbly voice. "I thought you were the delivery guy that brings our lunch." "No, just Grace and I," stated Tard. "May we come in?" "Yes, sure, of course, come on in." "Who is it dear?" asked Mr. Henderson. "You will have to come and see for yourself," responded Mrs. Henderson. "Can't you just tell me, I'm busy, I don't have time for any guessing games." Before Mrs. Henderson could answer, Tard walked into the study where Mr. Henderson was working. "Oh, it's no guessing game sir, it's just your daughter and son-in-law." "Mr. Henderson pushed back from his chair with an angry look in his eyes. Tard did not back down. Mrs. Henderson and Grace were just taking it all in. "What are you guys doing here?" asked Mr. Henderson. "By here, you mean what are we doing at my wife's parents' home?" "Are you being smart with me young man?" "That's right, I am a man. However, my age is irrelevant, but my stand as a man is solid. I brought my wife here to see and visit with her parents, are you going to be less than a man and turn her away?" "I don't appreciate your tone, and I have never turned Grace away from my home." "No, just the other half of her, and as for my tone, it doesn't seem to be any different than yours."

At that moment, Grace felt the need to intercept. "Hello father, how have you been?" "So, is that how it is now, you stand there and formerly greet me?" "Would you prefer that we walk over and embrace you?" "You are my daughter, of course I want to hug you." When Grace stepped closer towards her father, Tard intercepted. He walked up to Mr. Henderson and threw his arms around his neck. "Good to see you sir." Mr. Henderson was caught off guard, but he immediately responded by returning the affection. He threw his arms around his son-in-law's shoulders and gave him a big squeeze. "It is so good to see you son, and welcome." Tard was not surprised, but Grace was astonished. She stood looking at her husband and dad locked in an embrace as if she was frozen. When she was able to gain her composure, she slowly walked over to where the two stood. Mr. Henderson reached over to pull her into the circle. With tears streaming down his face, he said; "come on over here and give your old fool of a daddy a hug." She didn't hesitate, she fell into her father's arms, and like him, began crying. It was now Mrs. Henderson's time. She was the hardest cookie in the bag. She looked on at her family as if someone had lost their mind.

"Come on Diane, what are you waiting for?" asked Bradley. If Grace was astonished, Diane was horrified. "I am trying to figure out what is happening, am I supposed to be a part of that?" Tard stepped a few feet away from Mr. Henderson and asked Diane; "a part of what? Diane." "Whatever that is you all have going on over there. Well, no offense, but count me out." "Okay," said Tard, you're out." "So, Mr. Henderson can you take a lunch break right now?" asked Tard. "Sure, I can, just give me a minute." Mrs. Henderson was shocked that Tard dismissed her so easily, and asked; "did you really just dismissed me?" "No mam I didn't, you dismissed yourself." "Just what are you saying?" You are being disrespectful in my home. That is exactly the reason why I never wanted you in my daughter's life." Tard looked at Mrs. Henderson with sadness. "I am leaving right now, both my wife and I, and we are taking her father with us, so you can reset, or whatever it is that you do."

Mr. Henderson had tied up his loose ends and was ready to go to lunch with his daughter and son-in-law. He did not hear the end of Tard's and Diane's conversation. "Are you coming, dear? He asked Diane. "No, I'm not, and quite frankly, I don't understand why you are going." "Did you not hear Tard asked us out to lunch?" "No, I heard him ask you." "That is because you didn't want to hug him." "Whatever Bradley, you go on and I will deal with you later." Up until now, Tard was doing all the talking, but after the comment Mrs. Henderson made about dealing with her father later, Grace felt the need to speak up. "What do you mean, you will deal with him later? You can't still be that vindictive and hateful after all this time." "You watch your mouth young lady, as I said to that toad of a husband of yours, I will not be disrespected in my own home." "Maybe we should just take daddy back to Atlanta with us and keep him there. I don't like the sound of that, you will deal with him later." "Since when did you become your father's protector?" "Does he need protecting mom?" "I am not going to stoop to your level and answer that." "You don't have to ma; you really don't have to." "Come on guys, let's go, the sooner I get out of her, the better." Mr. Henderson didn't like the way things were going between the family. "Okay, wait a minute you guys' Diane is my wife and we support each other. I think it's only fair that she comes along as well. She's just upset because you didn't ask her initially. Come Diane, put you fangs in and come on, it's not every day that we get to see our children." Diane wanted to ask, what children, but instead, she said; let me grab my purse." Everyone gasped as Diane walked into the room and picked up her purse. "Ready?" she asked.

No one said a word as Diane walked past them and headed for the door. She didn't look back, nor did she ask what vehicle they would be travelling in. Once outside, she walked over to Tard and Graces's rental car and stood by the passenger door. Everyone else followed suit. Tard hit the remote to unlock the doors, and Diane pulled open the left back passenger door and crawled in. Bradley climbed in on the other side, while Grace and Tard stood outside steering at each other. They both made a hunch on their shoulders and crawled inside as well. "So, asked Mr. Henderson, where are we headed?" "I discovered this little restaurant not far from you on the way here and wanted to try it, said Tard; is there somewhere else you would like to go?" "No, wherever you take us will be fine. My wife and I seldom eat out, so we are not choosy."

Tard drove up to a quaint little restaurant with a blue storefront. "We're here." He got out of the vehicle and walked around to the front passenger's side and helped his wife out, before helping Mrs. Henderson. When Tard opened her door, she stuck one leg out before extending her hand for his assistance. Tard was glad to help, he was holding no grudges, he just wasn't taking any mess. When everyone had exited the vehicle, he put his arm around his wife's waist and headed towards the restaurant entrance. "Be careful honey, watch your steps." Mrs. Henderson was watching every move that Tard made and was beginning to be impressed. "Ok Tard, asked Mr. Henderson, what's the occasion?" "Well Mr. Henderson there is an occasion, and as soon as we all settle down, Grace will tell you what it is. Mr. Henderson was a little concerned that something might be wrong. In all the years that his daughter and Tard were married, he had never put forth the effort that he had on today. He began to think the worst. Mrs. Henderson was not without worry either. She was confused as to the reason Tard was so assertive with both Bradley and herself. She thought to herself, "I wonder what it could be, I pray they are not sick."

The server came and took their orders, and asked what they would like to drink. After the drinks arrived, Grace spoke up. "Mom, dad, I know that you do not approve of my marriage to Tard. When you refused to attend my wedding, that was the most painful day of my life. It took a lot of love and tender caring from my husband to help me overcome it. Tard is a great man, and a great husband. I could not have done any better if you guys had hand picked him yourselves. With that being said, we are all claiming to be Christians, but something is not lining up. As Christians, we should be able to put our differences behind us and forgive one another. I have forgiven you for not attending my wedding and for all the mean and hateful things you said about my husband, even today mom. I forgive you for not inviting us to holiday celebrations and meals. I would ask you to forgive me, but I don't know what it would be for. If you have an issue with me other than my marital choice, I will be glad to apologize."

The server had returned with their meals, and Grace stopped speaking. After their food was placed on the table and the server had left, Grace began speaking again. "Mom. Do you or dad have anything to say?" "You are the one that showed up on our doorsteps without warning, said Diane, why would we have anything to say?" Before Grace could respond, Bradley intercepted. "Yes Grace, I do have something to say; something I should have said a long time ago, but I allowed my pride to get in the way." "What is it dad?" "I want to say that I am so sorry for my past behaviors; I should have been at your wedding and should never have questioned your choice of husband. We taught you to make your own decisions, and when you did, we punished you for it. Can you ever find it in your heart to forgive me?" "As I stated earlier dad, I have already forgiven you. I had to, to be able to go on with my life, but if you need to hear the words, then I forgive you. I forgive you for all of it." With tears in his eyes, he thanked his daughter for all the pain he had inflicted upon her. After Grace had openly forgiven her father, he looked over at Tard; Tard, I am so ashamed. I am ashamed of the way I've treated you over the years without justification. I know that it's asking a lot, but if you can find it in your heart to forgive me, I would be forever grateful?" Tard looked at Bradley with a shy smile on his face. "Yes sir; I forgive you. I never wanted any of this and the only reason it bothered me at all is because it bothered my wife. We can put this behind us and begin anew." "Thanks son, you surely do have a heart of gold."

During the conversation between the others, Diane just sat and listened. "Why aren't you eating mom?"

asked Grace. "It is difficult to eat and talk at the same time." "But you're not talking." "Well, if you would give me half a chance I would." No one bothered to respond. Everyone at the table remained quiet; the only sounds were those of chewing and utensils against plates. Finally, Diane broke the silence; "Grace." "Yes mom." "A while ago you asked if I had nothing to say." "Yes, I did, but I got the impression that you didn't." "But I did; I have so much I want to say that I don't know where to start." "Well, I would jumpstart you, but frankly mom, I don't have a desire to dig up old bones, so you're on your own." "Mrs. Henderson took a deep breath, laid down her fork, wiped her mouth with her napkin, and began speaking. "Grace, like your father, I am ashamed of some of the ways I behaved towards you and Tard. I don't know who I thought I was. I wasn't born with a silver spoon, I had to work hard when I was a child, I never wanted that for you. That is why I went to college and made sure I had a great career so that I could provide for you the things that my parents were unable to give me. While I understand that is no excuse for my behavior, I just want you to see that even I am not perfect. I am truly sorry, so sorry; words alone are not even able to express how much. You are my only child, and I missed out on so much of your adult life. I missed your wedding and your college graduations. These are things I can never get back, but the sad part is, if I could do it over, I would probably do the same dumb things. It's just recently that my eyes began to come open, and I was able to let go of some of the bitterness of my heart. What you said touched me; if we are Christians our lives should line up as Christians. I guess all these years I was a pretend Christian. "So, what are you saying mom, I'm not sure I understand." One moment you seem to be apologizing and on the other you seem to be trying to justify your behaviors." "I know it looks that way, but please understand, this is difficult for me. I am not accustomed to acknowledging that I'm wrong. I accept responsibility for my behavior, and I do apologize. I am so sorry for all the pain I have caused you over the years, please forgive me." "Thanks mom, for your apology, I forgive you."

After receiving forgiveness from Grace, Diane turned her attention to Tard, and ask for his forgiveness. "What will forgiving you achieve? Just a little while ago, you accused me of being a toad and disrespectful towards you. Are you saying that you were wrong, and that you no longer see me as some low count bum as you so boldly put it?" Mrs. Henderson dropped her head and said, you're going to make me work aren't you." "Yes mam, I am not as easy going as Grace. I am her protector here on earth, and I must make sure that she is safe from every angle." "You don't have to worry or protect her from me, I am authentic in what I'm saying, it comes straight from the heart." "Then in that case, I forgive you from the heart." Tard got up and went over and hug Mrs. Henderson for the first time since he'd married her daughter." Everyone seemed to be of one accord. "I guess mission is accomplished," said Mr. Henderson. "Not quite sir," said Tard.

"What now, asked Mrs. Henderson, is there anything else that I need to do?" "No, said Grace, but there is something that I need to do." "What is it?" asked Mr. Henderson. Grace stood up and looked at her mom and dad. "Mom, dad, I want to say thank you; thank you for not being so high that you couldn't come down and accept responsibility for your mistakes. So, mission will not be achieved until I tell you this." She pulled her shirt close to her body and said, you guys are going to be grandparents; Tard and I are pregnant." Mrs. Henderson's mouth flew open so wide until it almost locked. "Oh my, what a great day, what great news." "I knew it from the moment you walked through the door," said Mr. Henderson. "Why haven't you said anything?" asked Grace. "I didn't want to steal your thunder, and I wanted to hear it from your own mouths."

After dinner was over, Grace and Tard took her parents' home. "Are you going back to Atlanta tonight?" asked Mrs. Henderson. "No, we're not," said Grace; we have a room at the hotel and will be there until Monday morning" "Please stay with us for these few days, it will be so wonderful," said Mr. Henderson. "Yes, please do," said Diane, can't you checkout of the hotel without being penalized?" "Are you sure mom?" "I have never been surer of anything in my life." "Okay then, I will see what we can do." "I have an idea Grace, you stay here with your parents, and I will go to the hotel and get our belongings and check us out. Is that alright with you?" "Thanks Tard, that is perfect. I am a little tired, it has been a long and cathartic day."

When Tard returned from the hotel, Grace and her parents were on the patio laughing and sharing stories from over the years. It was a pleasant sight to see. He walked over to where his wife was sitting and asked if she was alright. "Yes, I am fine; for the first time in a long time, things are the way they should be." "I agree," said Diane. When I think of all the time I'v wasted, it breaks my heart, but thank God for now." "Mom don't worry about the past, we cannot get it back, but hopefully, we have all learned from the past and are able to carry the lessons with us into the future. I believe that all things carry a purpose, we just need to uncover it."

Grace and Tard spent the weekend bonding with the Hendersons. When it was time for them to leave, both grace and Diane burst into tears. "Mom, you know Atlanta is not that far away, you could be there within an hour," said Grace. "I know" said Diane, and don't be surprised when we show up at your door unannounced."

Everyone laughed, which made the departure much easier.

When Grace gave birth to her daughter Jackie, six months later, Diane was there, and stayed until the baby was two weeks old. Life for the Hendersons was good, until a few months later when Diane was diagnosed with cancer. She had not been seeing a doctor regularly, so the cancer was in an advanced stage when it was discovered. Grace was devastated and insisted that she take care of her mom. She took unlimited leave from work and went to Florida to be with her mother. Six months after her diagnosis of cancer, Mrs. Hill was gone. Grace never felt so much anguish but knew that her mom was in a better place. Watching her suffer day and night and not being able to help her feel better took a toll on her. Although it hurted her to her core when her mother left, she gave God thanks for taking her from her suffering. She knew that her mom died a true Christian and that she would see the beauty of heaven.

Grace always made it her mission to see good in every situation. She knew or at least believed that nothing happens randomly and without cause. Because of her positive outlook on life, she was a constant positive influence on Tard. He had begun to see life through her eyes. They raised their daughter to have the same values as theirs. She was a well-adjusted child and grew up to be quite a young lady. After she graduated from college with her undergraduate degree in psychology, she continued until she received her master's degree in business. One year after she finished graduate school, she got married to a gentleman she met in college. He seemed like a nice gentleman, and Grace didn't want to make the same mistake with him that her parents had made with Tard, so she never questioned Jackie about his background or his character. Jackie was married for only a year before giving birth to her daughter Zelia. Two years later, she gave birth to her son Damon. Jackie was a great mom and took her children to church every Sunday the way her mom did with her. Damon was a part of the music ministry and Jackie sang in the choir. Tard and Grace were two proud parents and grandparents.

One evening, Jackie came to her parents' home with her two children. She had her eyes covered with dark glasses which only looked suspicious because it was below 30 degrees outside. When grace questioned her as to the reason, she was wearing the sunglasses, she flopped to the chair and began crying. "Jackie, her mother asked, what's wrong, why are you in tears?" When Jackie opened her mouth, nothing came out. Three years old Damon said in a loud angry tone, my daddy hit my mommy in her eye, bad daddy." Mrs. Hill hurried over to where Jackie was sitting and pulled the glasses from her face. What she saw was more than disturbing.

"Tard, please come here, something has to be done." Because of the urgency in Graces's voice, Tard rushed into the room. He took one look at Jackie's eye and headed towards the door. "No Tard let's do this the right way. We need to take her to the hospital so they can check her out." Against his better judgment, Tard went along with Grace's request. While at the hospital, Tard called the police and had Jackie tell him what had taken place at home. She explained that her husband Danny had been abusing her since before Zelia was born. She thought it would get better because he always apologized after he'd beaten her and asked for her forgiveness. But tonight, he started to hit Zelia, and I intercepted. I got the lick that was intended for my baby. This was the last straw," Tard and Grace were in shock at what had been happening to their child under their noses and they had no clue." "That's it said Tard, you are not going back to that apartment. You and the children are staying here with your mother and me." Since their little one-bedroom apartment in their early marriage, Tard and Grace had purchased a fifty-six square feet seven-bedroom home, so they had plenty of space. "I now know why we bought such a large house" said Tard to his wife. "I told you, everything has a purpose, said Grace."

After Danny was arrested and sent to prison, Jackie purchased a home for herself and her children. As much as she loved living with her parents, she wanted her independence. So, after eight months of living with her parents, she moved her family into their new home. Since their homes were within walking distance of each other, Grace saw her daughter and grandchildren often. Jackie seldom made a meal because Grace would cook for them most days. That was the life for them. Several years after moving into her new home, Jackie began leaving the children more and more with Grace, and Tard. When Grace asked her about it, she would just hunch her shoulder and ask. "You don't want to see your grandchildren?" "Jackie, you know that is not what I'm saying, but you are way out there in the fast lane. You need to rein it in." Grace's talk with Jackie had the opposite effect; although the children were now older, they were still minors and needed their mother. Some weeks she wouldn't see the children at all." It was during one of those absent times when Grace received the worse phone call of her life.

Tard was in a terrible accident on his way home from work and was airlifted to the hospital. Here Grace was with two children and no Jackie. She tried calling Jackie but was unsuccessful. She went over to her neighbor's house and explained what was going on and asked if they would watch the children. Mr. and Mrs. Scott were more than glad to watch Zelia and Damon. They were no longer babies and could almost take care of themselves. Grace was too nervous to drive herself to the hospital, so she called a cab to take her. When she arrived, she rushed into the emergency room, as the doctor that examined Tard was walking towards her. "Are you Mrs. Hill?" he asked. "Yes, I am, how's my husband?" "I am sorry Mrs. Hill but it doesn't look good; would you like to see him?" "Yes, please, I want to see my husband." "Before I let you in, I want to prepare you, what you see is not going to be pretty." Grace felt faint, but she braced herself and walked upright into the little room where Tard was laying. He was connected to so many machines that she could barely see him. When she walked into the room, he began moaning. "Come closer Grace, come closer, I need to tell you something." Grace walked closer to the bed as if someone or something was pushing her. When she approached the bed, she took her husband's bloody hand in Her's and said, yes dear, what is it?" He looked at her with painful eyes and said, "I love you." With a hoarse voice, she whispered, "I love to too Tard, so very much."

"I am not going to make it Grace, but I want you to remember, there's a purpose honey, there's a purpose. Tell Jackie and the children I said goodbye and that I love them with all my heart," "I will tell them Tard." "Good by Grace, I will see you in heaven." Grace bent down and kissed his swollen lips; "good by my love, I will meet you at the gate." Tard took a deep breath and his head fell to the side.

When Grace walked out of the room where Tard lie, her neighbors, the Scotts, were standing in the waiting room with the children. Grace knew that she had to show bravery for the sake of the children. "Hey grandma, said Damon; where is grandpa?" "Grandpa has gone to heaven." Both Zelia and Damon began screaming to the top of their lungs. It took everything grace had within her to keep from joining them. She thought about all the wonderful years they spent together, and all the great times they shared. She didn't feel that life had cheated her of anything. She was grateful for the sort of life that many people only dreamt about. She wrapped the children in her arms and began rocking them from side to side. When she had calmed them down a little, she asked the Scotts if they would take them home. The question became, where is Jackie and how do I tell her what has happened to her father. Jackie was a daddy's girl.

When Grace got home from the hospital, the children had all cried out. They were exhausted so grace sent them to bed without having to shower. She went into her room and sat on her side of the bed. She was numb and unable to shed a tear. She kept hearing Tard's voice saying "remember, there's a purpose, and I will see you in heaven." She just sat there twisting her hands. Suddenly her bedroom door flung open; It was Jackie. "Mom, why are you blowing up my phone? I am just trying to find some balance in my life, but you keep trying to keep tabs on me. I am a grown woman. If you don't want to keep the children that's fine, they are old enough to stay home alone now." Grace slowly looked up at Jackie, she couldn't believe her ears. What had happened to her child, why was she so far off the grid. At that moment, she could no longer contain herself. She burst into uncontrollable tears. "Mom, oh my god mom, I didn't mean to upset you, said Jackie, I'm so sorry, where's dad?" Grace just kept on weeping as Jackie continued to apologize. She didn't know how to break the news to her daughter that her beloved father had passed away. "Sit down Jackie, I have something to tell you." "Mom, you're scaring me, where's my children, are they alright?" "The children are asleep, they are alright." "Then what is it?" "Sit down Jackie." "I don't want to sit down mom, what is it?" "Jackie, sit your behind down now!" Jackie sat on the side of the bed and looked over at her mom. She had the same look on her face as she did when her grandmother had died. "Mom, where is dad, is he ok?" "Yes and no." "What do you mean yes and no, mom please!" "Yes, he's spiritually fine, but no, he is not physically fine. Your daddy has gone to heaven." Jackie stood up and stared at her mother for a second, then like a light switch, she was out. Grace didn't know what to do, but the noise from Jackie's fall woke the children. They came running in and were able to help Grace get Jackie of the floor and on to the bed. The fact that Jackie had consumed a considerable amount of alcohol did not make things any easier.

Grace began shaking Jackie and calling her name, trying to revive her, but she did not respond. After a few seconds had passed and Jackie was still out, Grace asked Zelia to hand her the bottle of water that was sitting on the table. Zelia did as she was told and brought the water to Grace wondering what she was going to do with it. When she handed her grandmother the bottle, she opened it and poured it on Jackie's face. When the cold water touched her face, she gasped and opened her eyes. She looked at her mom standing there with Zelia and Damon standing beside her and realized that she was not dreaming, and that her father really was gone. Without saying a word, she passed out again. This time, trying to resuscitate her was more difficult than before. Grace splashed more water on her face, without success, there was no response. Grace became fearful, so she gave Jackie a forceful shake, but still no response. "Zelia, hurry, call 911, now!" Zelia did as she was told in record time, then ran back to assist her grandmother with her mom. Damon was just standing there looking at his mom. He could not believe what was happening, first grandpa, now his mom.

    The ambulance arrived shortly after they received the call. After they examined her, they explained to Grace that her blood pressure was high, and they were concerned because she was still unconscious. They placed Jackie on the gurney and headed outside. The paramedics continued working with Jackie until finally, about halfway to the hospital, she responded by opening her eyes. "Where am I," she asked? "You are in an ambulance headed to the hospital; can you answer some questions for me?" Jackie did not want to answer any questions, she wanted answers. "Yes," she responded. After Jackie reaffirmed her name and birthdate, she asked, "why are you taking me to the hospital?" "Just to be on the safe side mam; your blood pressure is sky high and is not coming down." Jackie laid her head back down on the pillow from when she raised it to speak. She didn't say another word.

Jackie was taken to the same hospital that her father had died in just a few hours earlier. For the second time that day, Grace had to ask her neighbor to sit with her grandchildren while she went to the hospital. Mrs. Scott agreed to sit with the children but asked her husband if he would drive Grace to the hospital. "Stay with her now, she's going to need a ride back home." Mr. Scott and Grace headed back to the hospital with Grace praying all the way. When they arrived at the hospital, Jackie was lying on a gurney in a small room in the emergency room. When she got closer to her bed, a doctor stepped from behind the drape. "Doctor, asked Mrs. Hill; is she going to be alright?" The doctor recognized Grace her from earlier, and asked, Is the patient related to you?" "Yes, responded Grace, she's my daughter, my only child, is she going to be alright?" "Yes mam, I have no doubt that she will be ok, once we get her blood pressure stabilized; does she have a history of high blood pressure?" "No, she has always been as healthy as a horse." "Do you have any idea what may have caused it to suddenly climb so high?" Grace was fighting to hold back tears, but the dam broke, and she began to weep. The doctor escorted her to a chair and a nurse rushed and began telling the doctor something. After a few seconds, the doctor returned to Grace and said, mam, I am so sorry for what you are going through, but if it's any consolation, I will personally see to it that your daughter is fine." "Thank you doctor, but I think I must tell you that Jackie has been drinking. I don't know how much alcohol she consumed, but it may have contributed to the shock of losing her father tonight." "Thanks for the information, but we have already tested her alcohol level, it was not very high." Grace was relieved, at least that wouldn't be an issue.

After the doctor had thoroughly examined Jackie, he gave her some medication to control her blood pressure and an antidepressant to calm her down. When her pressure came down to a safe level, he released her to go home. Jackie, grace, and Mr. Scott returned to Grace's home where the children and Mrs. Scott were waiting. When Jackie walked into the room where the children were, they jumped up and ran into her. "Mom we were so afraid," said Zelia. "I am so sorry that I put you guys through this, but when mom told me that dad, well you know; I couldn't take it, I still can't." She looked over at her mother who was sitting quietly in a corner and said, "mom, I am so sorry; I can't even imagine what you must be feeling right now." Grace just twisted her hands and smiled while a tear dropped from her eye. "Mom, can you please tell me what happened, I just need to know. Do you feel up to telling me now?" "Your father was involved in a vehicle accident, and he did not survive the crash. I got to see him, and he told me that he loved me, and told me to tell you and the children that he loves you too. He smiled and told me that he will see me in heaven, and then he was gone." Grace got up from where she was sitting and placed her arms around her daughter's neck, and the two cried together until the morning."

After Grace had laid Tard to rest, she wondered how she would function without him. Her mother was gone, and her father was dating again. She knew that he'd had some rough days with her mother and wanted to protect him from similar situations. He was still a very handsome man, and a wealthy one at that. She didn't want anyone taking advantage of his vulnerability, but she wanted him to find happiness. She checked on him often and every chance she got, she visited with him. When Tard died, he came and spent six months with her, to help her get her footing back. When he left to go home, to keep from missing him so much, and falling into some type of depression, she spent her time caring for her family and doing community work. She was also a regular church attender. Before Tard's death, she sang on the choir, and took parts in other auxiliaries activities, but due to her grief and other responsibilities, she had very little time for rehearsals, so she stepped down from them. She still attended church, and she never lost her faith, just her motivation. She maintained that there is purpose to everything that takes place, and that beauty often blossomed from painful situations. Although she loved attending church, she had not been in a while due to her own health issues.

One year after Tard's death, Jackie and Zeila was in a head on collision by a drunken driver. They were both injured and had to be transported to the hospital by ambulance. Grace felt that she was reliving the same nightmare that she had when Tard was killed in an automobile accident. She spent days and nights helping Jackie and Zekia. Although both suffered severe injuries, Jackie's was worse. When Jackie was released from the hospital, she was sent to a rehabilitation center for physical therapy. After months of physical therapy and other treatments, they were both left to face a lifetime of pain. Jackie was unable to live the carefree lifestyle that she had adopted when she had divorced her husband. Some days she could barely get out of bed. She had become somewhat bitter and resentful. Although her parents had raised her up in the church, she only went occasionally. She had the voice of an angel but refused to sing in the church choir.

At times, Grace felt as if she was fighting a losing battle with her daughter, but she did not intend on giving up. She decided that things were not going to get any better if she didn't put forth the effort, so despite her health issues, she decided to return to church full-time. Her first Sunday back was emotional. She had given her testimony that she was back despite the devil trying to keep her away. She attempted to explain how the death of her family members, and her current health condition were her reasons for her slothful attendance. "But in all fairness" stated Grace, I allowed Satan to whisper into my ears, convincing me that these were valid excuses to stay away. I realize that no one feels good all the time, but we should use those times for growth and not as excuses or self-pity. Yes, I'm guilty, I went before my God in prayer and asked for his mercy and for his healing, and he granted me those things, but my human weakness gave in to the convictions of the devil. Although God had healed me, I was still holding on to the thought that I was sick. I want you to hear me now. Not all sickness ends in death, and not all death is because of sickness. There will be times when affliction will fall upon you in spite of all your good work and good intensions. Do not allow those trial times cause you to lose faith or hope. Instead, let your hope expand, let your faith strengthen, you can't do it alone, ask God to strengthen you in every way that you need strength. I realize that I have been physically absent from the church house for a while, but I have not been absent from God. So, as I give this testimony, don't look upon me with doubtful eyes, or disbelief, but see if you can see God within me and through me. See if you can identify with some of my testament and see if you may be uplifted by it. This is why I testify, not to be seen, but to be heard. Some of you are struggling within yourselves. Well, it's time you find peace. Ask yourself, what is the purpose of my circumstance? If you seek long and sincere enough, your answer will come. Once you receive your answer, your burdens will feel lighter, and your direction will become clearer."

    When Grace had finished her testimony, tears were streaming down her face, but they were tears of joy. The congregation stood and began applauding her. She looked from one member to the other; applause was not what she wanted, but she would have to start somewhere. When service was over, several members approached Grace and welcomed her back with open arms. Others thanked her for the inspiring message; and still others just embraced her. The pastor walked over to where Grace was speaking to a young lady; "Sister Grace, that was some testimony you gave. Before you left you were a powerhouse, and you returned, not only powerful, but full of wisdom and humility as well. Thank you so much because I for one needed that. I have been dealing with a lot of pain lately, both physical and emotional, but you gave me something to think about, something to feast on, again, thank you." "Reverend, if I was able to shed a little light, it was by the grace of God, but I thank you for keeping an open mind and for listening."

After speaking with the reverend, Grace decided it was time for her to go home, she was a little exhausted, and Jackie and Zelia were waiting at home for her. Her grandson Damon was the church drummer and had gone along with her to church. Jackie and Zelia had refused to go, and said they were in too much pain. "Come on

Damon, let's go home, grandma is feeling a little peaked." "Right behind you grandma."

After leaving church, Grace felt overwhelmed; although things had gone well at church, she still felt a little shaky. She sat on her chair, looked around the room and said aloud; "Wow! That was some service we had today. I am so glad that I decided to go even though I have been battling this old bad feeling for days." Her daughter, Jackie, who had been just outside the door, walked in and began speaking to her mother. "Mom, I still do not understand; I don't get why you felt the need to attend church when you are not feeling well." Grace, being the humble spirited person she was, just looked at her daughter and said, "well, yeah, you know, sometimes the day starts out rocky, but in the end, things get better." "So, is that how it played out for you today, Mom?" "What do you mean Jackie?" asked Grace. "Well, just looking at you from where I'm standing, I don't see better, so, can you clarify it for me so that I can see what you're seeing?" Grace looked at her daughter with a sad expression on her face. She wondered why Jackie was so skeptical and so negative most of the time. In the meantime, she felt the compelling need to respond and see if she could get her to see things from a different perspective. After careful thoughts, she responded by saying, "come on now, Jackie, that is not fair, every day is not the same, some days are much better than others, but you take the good with the bad." Jackie was not having it. She just was not having it. So, she looked at her mom, and in the calmest voice she could muster up, said; "mom, come on now?" "No, you need to come on! Said Grace. "Mom, that makes absolutely no sense to me and deep down you know it makes no sense to you either, you just keep fooling yourself." Grace rose from the chair she was sitting on and looked Jackie square in the eyes. Though she was slow to anger, Jackie had gone too far. She felt disrespected, angry, frustrated, and impatient. In an elevated voice, she said. "Wait a minute, Missy! Just what do you think you are talking about? Or whom do you think you're talking to? I am a Christian, but if you do not mind your tongue, I will make you swallow it." Jackie looked at her mom and said, "that didn't sound very Christian like to me." Grace looked over at her daughter in unbelief and asked her, "Jackie, are you really going there? What happened to you? Sometimes I barely recognize you lately. You walk around all day with your head in the sand and no one can ever tell you anything. It seems you want to be in a funky place. When I think about it, it seems you want to feel sad and unhappy and miserable. And because you do, it appears that you want to make everyone else around you feel the same way. It's at a point now that I find myself sometimes questioning who you've become." When

Grace had finished speaking, she sat back on her chair with her head resting in her hands.

Jackie looked at her mom with tears in her eyes. "Do I understand you correctly mom? Are you saying that you barely recognize me? Well, maybe God doesn't recognize me either. Maybe that's the reason he doesn't hear my prayers." "What is it Jackie that makes you question that God doesn't hear your prayers or hear you?" "Because he doesn't answer, he has never answered me. He can't answer if he hasn't heard me." "Have you considered that maybe he did answer and maybe you didn't like the answer or just didn't hear it?" As Grace and Jackie were talking back and forth, Jackie's daughter Zelia, burst into the room and asked her mom, who answered what?" Before Jackie could speak, Grace answered by saying Zelia, I'm talking with your mother; would you please just give us a moment?" Jackie decided to answer her daughter's question. "God." "Huh?" asked Zelia.

Grace jumped in and said OK, now let's not get her all excited, you know how she gets." Zelia looked at her grandmama with disappointment; "Grandma, I don't know if I like that statement, what do you mean how I get?" "Don't, let what mom said bother you Zalia, your grandmother is just a little naive at times." This did it for Grace; she threw her arms up in the air and walked out of the room grumbling to herself. "Lord, help my children."

Zalia was still curious and wanted to know what was going on between her mother and grandmother that had them so upset. She was used to seeing her mom in a downward mood, but her grandma was always cheerful and in an uplifting spirit. "So, what is it mom, what were you and grandma talking about? You never answered my question." "What question are you referring to Zalia?" "Come on, mommy, the question that you ask someone that did not get heard nor got answered." "Oh, I was just telling mom how God never hears or answers my prayers because he doesn't recognize me." "Oh really? yeah, I know what you mean, Mom. I have been praying about my situation as well. I ask God, why do I have to suffer so much pain? I'm still young. What happens to me when I am your age? It just doesn't seem fair. I'm unable to do most of the things that my friends do for fear of being hurt. I don't understand ma." "I wish that I had the answer for you, honey, I don't have any special connections to God. I have been praying for both of us, but I can't seem to get through."

Grace had managed to calm herself down and was returning to the room just in time to catch the end of the conversation between Jackie and Zelia. She looked affectionately at her daughter and granddaughter and with her normally controlled behavior, she lovingly said; "look children, there is a purpose for everything, just find your purpose." Jackie looked at her mom, she couldn't believe the words that were coming from her mouth. "Oh, come on, mom, come on now, what possible purpose could there be for all the pain my daughter and I are suffering?" "I don't know Jackie, but there must be one." "Well, when you find out what it is, please share it with me I would really like to know." "All I can tell you is that you need to continue praying day and night without ceasing." Before Jackie could respond, she began singing a song that she had written, and she sang it until she began nodding her head and tapping her feet. The title of her song was "I pray." She kept singing I pray, I pray, I pray. Jackie looked over at her mom and said, "what made you think that I haven't been praying? I told you I have prayed. I have been praying for years and I still suffer. So, it's not that I haven't prayed, it's that I haven't gotten any response to my prayers. Do you know what it feels like to be told that you have arthritis, Fibromyalgia, degenerative disc, neck pain and not to mention the emotional pain of having to suffer physical pain? And it's not just me, my child is suffering too, so what is the purpose in that?" "I understand, honey, but if you continue to pray and have faith, your changes will come." "Mom, with all due respect, I feel that this is my change, a change for the worse." After she said that, she walked out of the room leaving her mom speechless.

While Grace was still standing there as if she was frozen, her grandson Damon walked into the room. As he was entering, he noticed that something wasn't quite right with his grandmother, so he was looking at her with a curious expression. "What's wrong, grandma?" "I just don't know what to do, son." "Do about what?" "About your Mama." "What's wrong with Mama?" "If I could answer that question, I would be a millionaire, but if you asked her, something is wrong with me." "Did you play the lottery, Grandma?" "What are you talking about winning a lottery?" "You said you could be a millionaire, so I thought maybe you hit the lottery jackpot." "Boy hush your mouth and go sit down, that's the trouble with you young people, you don't listen, no one said anything about winning no lottery." "Well, I don't want to sit down, and why are you so grumpy today?" "It's your mom and sister." "What about mom and Zalia, what's going on with them that have you so upset?" "They don't seem to get that life just isn't no bed of roses; they don't seem to understand that we must suffer sometimes. Doesn't mean that we've done anything wrong, or that God doesn't have us in his favor. It doesn't mean that they have been targeted and they're the only ones that have issues or problems or suffering. They're complaining about pain; they can't see that the glass is half filled." "Grandma, I agree with Mom and Zelia, they have been suffering from pain for a long time now, and I heard mom praying and asking God to heal them. As I watched them, nothing seems to ever change if anything, they're getting worse. I know that you taught me that there is a purpose to everything, but grandma, what is the purpose of Mom and Zelia's pain, huh ma?" "Honey, you will understand it better one day. Not only is there a purpose, but beauty. Often, we can't see the beauty because we can't get pass the pain."

"Don't you have choir practice this evening? Yes, I do, and I'm looking forward to beating those drums, I just love it, but I'm also concerned about my mom and my sister, and I'm concerned about you too, Grandma. You seem to be allowing all of this to get to you; I know you have faith in God and I know you trust him, but you must remember that we are not where you are, we have to get there, Grandma, and so on that note, I think I'm leaving, because, as I said, I love beating those drums." "Yeah, and I love hearing you beat them too."

Jackie was returning to the room where her son and mother were having a conversation. She heard Damon telling his grandmother that he was leaving for rehearsal. "Yes, Damon, go on to rehearsal, although I don't know for the life of me why Jerry would have rehearsal on

Sunday evenings." Because it is when most members are available," replied Damon. "Well, make sure that you say a prayer for me while you're there, maybe God will hear you." "OK, Mom, I will beat the drums and pray for you and Zelia, I will pray for you to Grandma, and ask God to help you from being so naïve." "Child If you or your mom call me naive one more time, I am going to take that word from your vocabulary." "And how are you supposed to do that, Grandma?" "You don't want to know. Now go on to your choir rehearsal boy." Yes mam, I'm out." When Demon had cleared the room, Jackie looked over at her mom and asked, mom, why do you refuse to face reality?" Looking confused, Grace returned the question; "What reality would that be, Jackie?" "Never mind, Ma, you will never get it, I'm going to choir practice with Damon. I think that I am going to join. Maybe if I sing, God will hear me. Once I get his attention, I will ask him again to heal me from my pain and suffering." "It's good that you are joining the choir Jackie, and that you haven't completely lost your faith in God. Maybe on some level, it will help you to get a better understanding." "Yes, mam mommy dearest, whatever you say," said Jackie sarcastically, as she turned and walked out of the room. Grace was left with her mouth half open. She was unable to have the last word because Jackie had walked out and closed the door behind her.

Jerry Bridgeport was the choir director, and he was adamant about the members being on time. He would get so frustrated whenever they were late that he would chew them out, but as usual, some of the members were late. Jerry looked around at the ones that had made it on time and asked, "where are the others? I am so sick and tired of you guys always being late. If I can manage to get here on time all the time, seems to me you should be able to be on time at least some of the times." Denzel, one of the choir members spoke up and said, "well, maybe if we didn't have to rehearse so often, we would be inclined to be on time." "So often?" asked Jerry, so often?" "What on earth do you mean? If we had it any less, we simply wouldn't have it at all." "Why do we?" ask Denzel. "Why do we need rehearsal?" Jerry looked at Denzel as if he was a stranger. "You're kidding me, right? I'm not even going to answer that question." Clary, another member, agreed with Denzel. "It does seem like we are having rehearsing an awful lot, almost every Sunday, and sometimes during the weeks." "Pansy, also another member, jumped in and began defending the director. "OK, now let's be respectful. Jerry only has our best interest at heart." Again, Denzel disagreed; "no, he doesn't, the only thing he cares about is this choir. He lives and breathes choir." Pansy responded by saying "I wouldn't go that far as to say he doesn't care about us. Yes, he does love the choir, but he cares about us as well. He is very passionate about the choir and wants it to be the best that it can be."

By this time, Damon came strolling in late, waving his hand in the air as if he was in a Christmas parade, shouting, "reporting for choir practice duty." Jerry looked over at Damon and said, "So, Damon, tell me, do you feel like some of the others? Do you think that we rehearse too often?" "Heck no, I could beat these drums every day and it wouldn't bother me. The only reason that I'm late today because of my family issues." "Family issues, what's going on?" "Anything I can help with," asked Jerry?" Damon looked at Jerry and tried to decide if he wanted to share his family's dirty laundry with him. They were a private family, and he didn't know if his mom and sister would appreciate him disclosing the problems that they were having at the home, so he looked at Jerry and said, "well you know how my mom and my sister have been suffering the last several years due to different physical and emotional issues, well grandma is trying to convince them that there is some type of divined purpose for their suffering." "Oh yeah, and did she happen to say what those purposes are?" "That's just it, she doesn't know what, she just believes that there is." "You know that your grandma is a wise woman, but even I would be skeptical about finding some purpose in pain, especially If it's me that's painting." "Oh yeah, I forgot to tell you that my mom has decided to join the choir." "Do you think that she is up to it?" asked Jerry. "Yes, to be honest, I'm thinking that this may be exactly what she needs right now to help keep her mind off her conflictions." "Ok, she's welcome to join, but she won't be getting any special treatment from me. She will be held accountable just as everyone else."

When Jerry had finished listening to Damon's concerns about his family's health, he turned his attention back to the business at hand. "Okay guys, come on, let's get to rehearsing so that we can get out of here at a decent time." "Here he goes again, said Denzel, rehearsal, reversal, come on Jerry, I am rehearsed out." Jerry was now getting a little put out by Denzel's constant nagging about rehearsal frequency, so he said to him; "Denzel, it's like this, rehearse or walk, the choice is yours." In all the years that he had known Jerry, Denzel had never heard him so precise and authoritative. He sat and dropped his head without saying another word." "Well alright then, if anyone else has anything negative to say about rehearsal, I suggest you keep it to yourself, shall we begin."

"Hey yawl, what's up?" asked a hesitant Jackie, as she strolled into the rehearsal hall. "Hello Jackie, replied Jerry, I heard that you may be interested in rejoining our choir." "Yes, I may have my own agenda for joining though." "And what would that agenda be?" "I've been having trouble connecting with God, it seems he just doesn't hear me. I don't know if it's because I am not worthy because of things I have done in my life or if I'm just going about it in the wrong manner. Maybe if I join the choir, I will be able to get through to him." "Jackie, you do know that you don't need to join a choir to get through to God, don't you?" "No jerry, if I knew that, would I be joining?" "So, if I don't need to join the choir, you tell me, why has he not heard me, why has he not answered my prayers?" "What did you ask him for?" "I asked him to heal my child and me." "What will you do once he heals you?" "Huh?" "What would you do? Yes, you said you want to be healed from your pain and suffering, you said that God does not hear you, but I'm asking, what if God were to heal you right this minute, what would you do?"

While Jackie was staring at Jerry as if he was the dumbest person she'd ever seen, Grace walked in and said, "go ahead Jackie, answer the question, what would you do if God healed you this very instant?" "Mom, with all due respect, don't start on me again, I am at the end of my rope." "No, you're not, if you were at the end of your rope, you wouldn't be seeking answers. The question that Jerry asked you is powerful, think about it, what would you do?

Would you still join the choir, or would you feel that there's no need now? Jackie honey, you know that I love you and want whatever is best for you, but seriously, I do not always know what that is." "Are you saying that you don't believe that being pain free is best for me?" "What I believe isn't the issue, but I do think that you need to reassess your situation and ask yourself, is the glass half empty or is it half filled." "What does a half empty or half-filled glass have to do with this, as I stated before mom, you are so in denial."

Before grace could defend herself, Zelia entered the rehearsal hall. "My goodness, I came here to join the choir and here you two are at it again. Can't I ever be somewhere the two of you are not?" "That is the reason I'm here," stated Grace. When I heard Jackie talking about joining, I figured, why not, Jerry has been campaigning for new members for a while now." "So, because I said I was joining, you decided to come down here and continue harassing me, huh?" "No, I don't want to harass you, just sing for the Lord." "Oh, good," said Jerry, the way I see it the more the merrier, but as I told Damon concerning his mom, there will be no preferential treatment." "I'm not looking for any special treatment" said Grace, just glad to help." Jackie was playing the silent card and did not respond to Jerry's comment. "Ok then," said Jerry, time is money, let's get started." Everyone got on board, and the rehearsal was a success.

"Wow, what an amazing rehearsal," said Jerry. Thanks guys: Jackie I have no doubt that God heard your angelic voice, you sang your heart out." "Do you really think so Jerry?" "I have no doubt." "Maybe he did, I surely hope so; maybe this time I finally got through to him!" Jackie was excited and felt a sense of accomplishment. "I should have joined your choir a long time ago, maybe I could have saved myself a lot of heartache." Jackie kept humming to herself as Grace stepped up on the platform beside her.

"Great job Jackie, I keep telling you that God hears you. I told you that there's a purpose for your pain and discomfort. What I'm trying to get you to understand is that from every bad thing comes something good." "Ok mom, I'll bite; what is one good thing that has come from my pain and suffering?" "Let me enlighten you just a little. I need you to hear me out, not tune me out or label me as certifiable or naive, but as someone that has lived, experienced, and has a sense of understanding. I don't just speak from the air I breathe, but from the spirit I live, and from the inspiration I receive from the Father. I know you think that I am in some denial about reality, but if you would just shut your mouth and open your heart, you may learn a thing or two from this old naive lady." As Grace spoke, she caught the attention of the other choir members, including Jerry the director. "I am not standing here pretending to be holier than thou, nor do I profess to be perfect, but I didn't just live these seventy-seven years in vain. If I tell you that it's raining, you had better grab your umbrella. Are you ready to listen to me now without attitude?" "Go ahead mom, I'll do my best."

"Do you remember some of the things you did when you were pain free? Do you remember the life you lived? The pain has slowed you down and given you time to rethink your life, and that's a glass half filled." "Mom, are you suggesting that God is punishing me for my past mistakes?" "No Jackie, no, that is not what I am saying at all. I'm simply trying to get you to see not just physical pain, but emotional and spiritual pain as well. Your pain is not the punishment, but the blessing." "So, now my pain is blessing me; I mean, like wow mom; I know that blessings come in all shapes and sizes, but I never knew that pain fitted into that category. There's no doubt, you have completely lost your mind." "Say what you may Jackie, but the day you had that terrible accident was a blessing for you; you are able to see the world differently because you move slower. You can appreciate the times when you lived without pain; most of all, you have learned how to pray. What you need to do now is find your purpose. Ask God to guide you, to give you wisdom and understanding, and then listen and be patient."

"What about me grandma, asked Zelia, are my pain blessings too?" "What do you think Zelia?" "You heard what I said to your mom; well, the same thing applies to you. I'm not picking at your mom; I would say the same things to anyone in her situation?" "But my situation is different from mom's, she has lived much longer than I have. I don't know what issues she has with her life living; I am only sixteen, I haven't lived much." "You're missing the point Zelia, remember when I said that the pain is not the punishment, but the blessing?" "Yes, I heard you, although I don't quite understand what you mean." "Think about it without judgement and you will discover your answer."

Zelia stood silent for a few seconds, then looked at her mom and said, "now that I think about it grandma, I understand. The actual pain is not my blessing, but the wisdom I receive during my trials. I got it grandma, I got it. Satan has been trying to discourage me and caused me to dwell on my situation instead of realizing my purpose. Each time you attempted to get me to see the light, he would whisper into my ear, and tell me not to believe what you were telling me. So, I would believe that there is no purpose, and that God is punishing me for some reason, and that the punishment is the purpose." "Well, Satan is a liar, and I rebuke him in the name of Jesus." "Grandma, seriously though, maybe I jumped the gun a bit, I am so anxious to believe that there is some type of purpose to my seemingly endless suffering that I grabbed on to the idea that maybe there is, and maybe there's hope for me." "Zelia dear, never second guess yourself."

Zelia began reminiscing about the tug-a-war thoughts she had within herself. She remembered a dream that she had after one of her grandmother's lectures. Satan was trying to convince her that she was doomed to a life of pain and misery. In her dream, she was telling her mom that her pain couldn't possibly be a blessing, and that there was no other purpose to it than to punish her. She remembered Satan whispering into her ear and saying, "you're right girl, how could there possibly be any good coming from pain. Come on now, you're smarter than that.... I should know because I cause pain every single day to people all over the world. Do you think I want them to feel good? Come on, its pain." Zelia remembered that she had regained her convictions while talking with Satan. She looked him square in the eyes and said, "say what? You mean to tell me that it is you that is bringing all this pain and discomfort into my life, and I'm just allowing you to do so?" "Yep, you got it." "Well so long Satan, and goodbye."

"Zelia, where did you go?" asked Grace; are you alright?" "Yes grandma, I am finally alright, you are so right, I am no longer going to allow Satan to take away my hope." "That's the spirit, because truth be told, it was never God that caused your pain, it was Satan. God allowed him to conflict you because he knew that you would be able to carry the cross and be a rainbow for others. I am so proud of you Zelia, and how you were able to see things from all angles at your age. You are a pillar, and you will be an encouragement for others. Now if I can only get you mother to follow your lead." Tell me though, how did you come to see things so differently so quickly? Just a few minutes ago, you were self-doubting." Zelia told her grandma about the dream she had remembered where Satan was trying to convince her not to believe anything that she had told her. "Thanks grandma, thanks for reminding me of what is important. I will forever be mindful of my blessings and purposes in all my life's situations." Zelia bent down to where her grandma was now sitting and kissed her on the forehead; "thanks grandma, I love you so." "I love you too baby, let's go home."

Jackie was sitting quietly during the entire conversation between Grace and Zekia, but now she felt compelled to say something. "Hold up mom, before we leave to go home there's something I need to say." Grace was getting tired of Jackie's attitude and unwillingness to see things from more than one angle. She wanted to just keep walking, but instead, she stopped and in a sweet gentle voice, asked; "what is it Jackie, what do you want to say?" "As I sat and listened to you and Zelia and saw how my baby was able to get an understanding of what you were telling us, I felt really bad. I should have made more of an effort to listen to you. I am ashamed of my behavior. I am beginning to get a better understanding of what you have been telling me for months. There were times when I wanted to believe you, but it was easier to feel sorry for myself. I too allowed Satan to convince me that you were the one wrong, and that you didn't have a clue as to what you were saying. I should have known better. You have never steered me wrong, and I respect you so much. I am sorry for the ugly things I said to you." "Do you really see honey, because Lord knows I've been praying that you would allow God to open your eyes. I know it is not easy trying to find something positive within something negative, but there always is. And yes, I accept your apology." "Thanks mom, you know sometimes we are so fixated on the solution that we fail to see the actual purpose." "Yes, we do; Satan would have us believe that God doesn't hear or answer our prayers because we're not worthy but believe me when I tell you that Satan is a liar. What pleasure could God possibly get from seeing his children suffer?" "Thanks, mom, for your wisdom and for not giving up on me. You know, sometimes it gets so hard, and I feel as if I want to give up. It is hard trying to accept that there's positive purpose or beauty in anything that is causing so much havoc in my life. I appreciate you for encouraging me and helping me to change my perception and regain my faith in God." "It is all good baby, so let us get out of here and go home. There are things I want to share with all of you to further help you understand what I am saying, but I need some food in my stomach first."

Grace, her daughter Jackie, her granddaughter Zelia, and her grandson Damon walked out of the church together laughing and conversing. Most of the other choir members had already left, but Jerry had stayed behind to listen to what was being discussed. He had always respected Mrs. Hill, but today, he found a new level of respect for her and her family. "Excuse me Ms. Grace, but I wanted to tell you how impressed I am with what you just shared with your family. Although I personally have not experienced much physical pain in my life, I am sure that I will benefit from the information you gave, if not for me, for someone else." "Thanks Jerry, but I'm not trying to win a popularity contest, just trying to keep my family spiritually healthy and happy." "Would you like to come over for a late dinner? I made a family meal earlier, but with all the chaos, no one took the time to eat it." "I would love to Ms. Hill, but I had better get home before my wife sends a search party out for me." "Well, in that case you had better go on home, but feel free to come by any time and bring Debrah with you." "Yes mam, I will do that very soon."

The evening had gotten late when Grace returned home. Shortly after she entered her home, her daughter Jackie, and grandchildren Zelia and Damon came in behind her. She hurried to the kitchen and began rattling pots and pans. Pretty soon, she was calling everyone to come into the dining room for dinner. "Well, that didn't take long," said Jackie. "That's because everything was prepared, I just had to reheat them," said Grace. "So, grandma, asked Zelia; are you going to finish preaching to us?" "Was that what I was doing?" "Sort of seem like it," said Damon. Mrs. Hill burst into laughter, as she said, "bow your heads children, let's say grace." "You get that grandma, laughed Damon, let's say grace." Damon was always the clown in the family. Despite the seriousness' of the moment, they all burst into laughter. "Leave it to the menace to say something like that," laughed Grace.

Dinner was going well, everyone was enjoying their meals and talking about one thing after the other. After a few minutes had passed, Zelia couldn't stand it any longer; "grandma, you never answered my question." "What question Zelia?" "When you were talking about pain, and purpose at the church, it really had an effect on me, and you said that you would continue once you got some food in your belly; well, your belly looks quite filled now, so how about it grandma, will you share some more insight?" "I don't remember saying anything about my belly, but yes, now that you girls have regained your powers, I will be glad to shed a little further light on the subject." "Just how are you going to do that grandma?" asked Damon. "Let me start by saying, not only is there purpose through painful experiences, but there is also beauty at the end of it." "You are going to have to explain that one to me grandma, said Damon. I have gotten on board with you and the purpose but tell me, where's the beauty?" "Before I go into examples of the beauty of pain, let me just say this; You have been raised in church, and you learn how to read the bible at early ages. You attended Sunday school and Bible study, and you listened to the ministers preach on various subjects. You understand the books of the Bible and you know how to seek comfort for whatever your needs may be. Well let me take you back to the book of

James, chapter 1; verses 2-4, that says "suffering produces growth and maturity." When we turn to God during our pain, he can use our suffering to mature our faith. Now, if you truly believe those words, you would not be able to dismiss the idea that suffering produces beauty and maturity of the spirit." "I hear what you are saying grandma." "I have read that scripture many times but didn't really understand what it meant, hearing you explain it, it makes more sense," said Jackie.

"Let me share a few more scriptures with you, and maybe it will strengthen my approach," said Grace. You don't have to do it tonight, but the first chance you get, I want you to read these Bible verses." Grace began quoting bible scriptures and verses. "Wait a minute mom, you're going too fast, let me get a pen and jot them down, otherwise, I won't remember them all," said Jackie. "There's no need for all of us to take notes, mom, you can make copies for Zelia and me, won't you?" asked Damon.

"Sure, I will," said Jackie. Grace continued spitting out Bible verses that could help her family maneuver through their physical and spiritual afflictions. "Okay, I will slow down, but I will only give you the verses, you are going to have to look them up and ask God to give you understanding as you read them." "Fair enough mom, fair enough." Say, grandma, once we have finished reading all of them, can we meet and discuss them just to see how well we understand and are able to apply them to our lives?" asked Zelia. "Now that's a smart girl right there; sure, we can, that is a wonderful idea." "Okay, here they are Jackie, take notes." Jackie began writing as her mother called out various bible verses.

**1 Peter 2:19-21:** "For this is a gracious thing, when, mindful of God, one endures sorrows while suffering unjustly. For what credit is it if, when you sin and are beaten for it, you endure? But if when you do good and suffer for it you endure, this is a gracious thing in the sight of God. For to this you have been called because Christ also suffered for you, leaving you an example, so that you might follow in his steps."

**1 Peter 4:12-19**: "Beloved, do not be surprised at the fiery trial when it comes upon you to test you, as though something strange were happening to you. But rejoice insofar as you share Christ's sufferings, that you may also rejoice and be glad when his glory is revealed. If you are insulted for the name of Christ, you are blessed, because the Spirit of glory and of God rests upon you. But let none of you suffer as a murderer or a thief or an evildoer or as a meddler. Yet if anyone suffers as a Christian, let him not be ashamed, but let him glorify God in that name. ...

**1 Peter 5:10:** "And after you have suffered a little while, the God of all grace, who has called you to his eternal glory in Christ, will himself restore, confirm, strengthen, and establish you."

**Romans 5:3-5:** "Not only that, but we rejoice in our sufferings, knowing that suffering produces endurance, and endurance produces character, and character produces hope, and hope does not put us to shame, because God's love has been poured into our hearts through the Holy Spirit who has been given to us."

**Romans 8:18:** "I consider that our present sufferings are not worth comparing with the glory that will be revealed in us."

**Psalm 23:1-6:** "The Lord is my shepherd; I shall not want. He makes me lie down in green pastures. He leads me beside still waters. He restores my soul. He leads me in paths of righteousness for his name's sake. Even though I walk through the valley of the shadow of death, I will fear no evil, for you are with me; your rod and your staff, they comfort me. You prepare a table before me in the presence of my enemies; you anoint my head with oil; my cup overflows.

**Psalm 34:18:** "The Lord is near to the brokenhearted and saves the crushed in spirit."

**Psalm 119:71:** "It is good for me that I was afflicted, that I might learn your statutes."

**Isaiah 30:20-21:** "And though the Lord give you the bread of adversity and the water of affliction, yet your Teacher will not hide himself anymore, but your eyes shall see your Teacher. And your ears shall hear a word behind you, saying, "This is the way, walk in it," when you turn to the right or when you turn to the left."

**2 Corinthians 1:3-4:** "Blessed be the God and Father of our Lord Jesus Christ, the Father of mercies and God of all comfort, who comforts us in all our affliction, so that we may be able to comfort those who are in any affliction, with the comfort with which we ourselves are comforted by God."

**2 Corinthians 4:17:** "For this light momentary affliction is preparing for us an eternal weight of glory beyond all comparison."

**Hebrews 2:10:** "For it was fitting that he, for whom and by whom all things exist, in bringing many sons to glory, should make the founder of their salvation perfect through suffering."

**James 1:12:** "Blessed is the man who remains steadfast under trial, for when he has stood the test he will receive the crown of life, which God has promised to those who love him."

"Okay mom, how many more?" asked Jackie. "Oh, I have plenty more, but I'll stop there, that is a good start," replied Grace. "Mom, I never realized that there were so many verses in the bible referring to suffering," said Jackie. "Yes, whatever you need answers too or comfort for, you can find them in God's words." "Thanks for the scriptures mom, but that doesn't get you off the hook," said Zelia with a grin on her face. "And just why am I on the hook Zelia?" "You promised to give us examples of purpose and beauty of pain and suffering." "I did, didn't I?" I was so caught up in giving you the right verses for the accession, that it slipped my mind. Let me see where I shall start." "The last thing I remembered you saying grandma, was not only is there purpose to pain, but that there is also beauty in pain," said Damon. I don't think that I said that there is actual beauty in pain; pain itself is not a beautiful thing, but what I said is that there is beauty at the end of it." "Just as you seek for your purpose, you must acknowledge your blessings. If you don't you will just take things for granted, and never be grateful for the blessings or the lessons. So often we feel entitled, and as a result, we become selfish and self-centered." "Now that I've said that, let me share with you a few examples of how pain produces beauty." "Okay mom, I am all ears," said Jackie.

Grace hesitated for a few seconds, she wanted to carefully choose her scenarios so that they would clearly be able to see what she had been telling them. "Ok, now I think that we are all on the same page concerning purpose, am I right?" "Yes mam," was the reply from each person in the room. "Ok, great! I will start with a short story about a twenty-eight-year-old woman. For nine months she carried a little baby girl in her womb. Sometimes she was nauseous; sometimes her feet were swollen and painful, sometimes, her back pained so badly seemed like it would literally snap in half, but she bared those pains gladly, because she had a purpose. To top it all off, came the day of delivery, and you talk about pain; those delivery pains; and boy did she ever labored. For three days she labored with pain so intense, they seemed almost unbearable, but she kept her focus and continued to trust in God and then...." Before she could get another word out of her mouth, Jackie interrupted. "And then came the rainbow." Grace continued; "Yes Jackie, and then came the rainbow. The most beautiful bundle of joy imaginable. The pain was soon forgotten, but the joy and beauty of it all is standing here in front of me." "Mom, that is such a sweet story. I never knew that you stayed in labor so long with me," said a teary-eyed Jackie. "Yes, and I would do it all over again if I had to, you are so worth it, and my what beauty." "Thanks mom, I love you too."

"That was deep grandma, and I get the point, I think, but can you give us another example?" asked Zelia. "Of course, I can; I loved my mother with all my heart, and I watched as she suffered with pain caused by cancer endlessly. I would hear her praying and asking God to take her home. I was being selfish, because I wanted to keep her as long as possible even though she was suffering. Then, one day God called her home and the pain in my heart seemed like it would last forever." "What beauty came from that grandma?" asked Damon." "The beauty of freedom! Freedom! Freedom from all the suffering from this world, and the beauty of Heaven and the Lord." "But grandma, what was the purpose of her suffering in the first place?" "Blessed is the man who remains steadfast under trial, for when he has stood the test he will receive the crown of life, which God has promised to those who love him: **James 1:12**." "Have you ever heard the expression, "no pain, no gain?" Whatever her purpose was, she found it. It was not for me to know, but for her to know."

"Okay mom," said Jackie, I see the beauty of your labor and of grandma's suffering, and you are absolutely right. Now, I clearly see this beauty of life. Before I was struck with all this pain, I was carefree and nonchalant, thinking only of myself and the desires of my heart. I took life and God for granted. Because of the pain though, I had to slow down, and in doing so I'm able to see through the eyes of others. Just the other day, a friend of mine was in a terrible car accident and stated that she does not want to live in such pain. Now I will be able to share the wisdom that you gave me with her. Knowing that I will be able to do that for her is because of the things you told me, and I was moving slow enough to hear it. There was a time when I would not have stood still long enough to have the conversation, let alone engage in it. But here I am, able to minister to someone else, it feels good; thanks."

"Jackie there's something else you have forgotten." "What's that mom?" "After your accident and you lost your job and was put on disability, you received several types of benefits, but one in particular, do you remember what it is?" "Yes, I received Medicaid insurance, and several other types of benefits?" "Yes, but do you remember the really beautiful ones, the big one?" "I'm not sure mom, what ones are you referring too?" "Don't you remember how you were struggling to pay off your student loans? You would have been paying them for most of your life, but what happened?" "Oh my God, how could I have forgotten, all of my student loans were forgiven, now that is beautiful, ma, a blessing straight from heaven."

"Yeah grandma," said Zelia, that reminds me of my girlfriend's mom. She lost her home and all her belongings during the storm. She was in such pain that I wept with her. But guess what grandma? Even though she lost everything, before the storm, her home needed a lot of repairs, and her furniture was old and worn. But after the storm destroyed her old stuff, she was able to file a claim with some disaster organization, and received a brand-new home, fully furnished. I was even a little envious of all her new stuff. Just when she thought she didn't know what she was going to do, God stepped in and rescued her, if that ain't beautiful I don't know what is. There were times grandma when I thought you were ludicrous and flew right out of the coo-coo nest." "Say what?" asked Grace. "Wait a minute grandma…. I sometimes didn't believe you, but it was because I did not understand. Now that I do, I can tell her that there was purpose in her loss and beauty from her pain. I can tell her to hold on to her faith with all her strength." "Oh, because I was just about to give you an inch of my mind. Laying jokes aside Zelia, you are one wise teenager. Many young people your age would not have entertained my constant blabbing but would have walked away without understanding. I appreciate you."

"Yes, and if my friend's mom has any questions concerning pain and purpose, I am going to tell her to ask my grandma." "Grandma, I may have jokes, but I am so grateful for you, not everyone is blessed to have a grandma with your wisdom. I could have lived my whole life without knowing what I learned from you, what a gift." Zelia bent down and kissed her grandmother on the cheek and gave her a big hug.

"Yes girls, I am just thankful to God that my girls are beginning to see the half-filled glass instead of dwelling on the half empty. I truly believe that you girls have found your purpose through your sufferings and have realize that the beauty that comes as a result of your pain and suffering, is as radiant as your rainbow!"

"Okay Damon, I've heard from the girls, tell me, what are you thinking, you have been quiet." "Grandma, I just sat and listened to you, mom, and Zelia. Each time one of you spoke, I gained a little more understanding. But most of all, it did my heart good to see that my mom now realizes that God has not sorted her out to punish her, but that he has heard her, and that he loves her. I have watched my mom and sister suffer for a long while, and every day I wondered what I could do to help them. Now it seems that they may be on the road to recovery." "And did you get all of that today?" "Yes, mam, I did. Before, I was like Zelia, I thought that you were just talking out the sides of your mouth but didn't have a clue as to what you were saying. You caught my attention at the church. I guess choir practice really did come in handy, huh?" "Boy you are wiser than I imagined; continue to love and support your mother and sister, one day you are going to make someone a great husband, and father." "Well thanks grandma, but that's a long way off." "I sure hope so, because as smart as you are, you're still just a boy."

"If I could get some help in putting away all this leftover food and cleaning this kitchen, I have another story I will tell, that will out top any other story you have ever heard," said Grace. "Another story grandma asked Damon. Is it a true story?" "Yes, it is; it is the truest story that you will ever hear in your lifetime. But the thing is, you have heard this story told before, many times. Once I tell it to you again, you will truly see how the dots connects." "Why don't you go ahead and tell us grandma, asked Zelia, I want to hear it." "I will tell you, but not before this kitchen is cleaned and all foods have been put away." "Come on Damon let's help grandma clean up, she thinks she's is smart." "I am smart, and to sure you just how smart I am, let me know when you're finished, I'm going and take a load of my feet." "Now that's telling them ma," said Jackie laughing as loud as she could." Zelia and Damon looked at their mother as if they wanted to punish her but knew better. "Okay mom, it's not that funny," said Zelia. "Oh, but it is, responded Jackie." "Would you like to know what's even funnier?" asked Grace. "What?"

"Jackie, you help them to make sure everything is done correctly, I don't want no mess in my kitchen, and call me when you're done, I will be nodding on this chair." Without a response, Jackie turned, followed the children to the dining room and began clearing the table. Zelia and Damon knew not to say another word, Jackie was ruffled.

When all the food had been put away and the kitchen sparkling, Jackie and the children went in the family room to wake Grace who was sleeping comfortably on her recliner. When Damon attempted to wake her, Jackie shushed them to be quiet. "She's had a long day, let her rest, we can hear the story another time." Both children agreed with their mother as they gathered their belongings and headed for home. Once outside, Jackie looked over at her children with pride. She was so happy that they made parenting so pleasant. She began smiling and crying all at the same time. "What's wrong mom why are you crying?" asked Damon. "These are happy tears son. I am just so happy that no matter how far I got off the rail, you guys stayed true to yourselves. When I was mentally unable to be nurturing to you, you never gave up on me. I thank God for the two of you every day, and I thank momma for stepping up and filling in when I wasn't available. From now on, things are going back to normal; actually, they are going to be better than normal. I have a tool now that I didn't have before." "What's that mom?" asked Zelia. "I have the tool of knowledge and understanding, and a little bit of wisdom. I have something to build on. I am never going to allow myself to go back to that dark place. There was nothing there but sadness and self-pity, and I am better than that." Zelia, because of me, you were headed in the same direction that I was in but thank God through the eyes of one wise Grace Hill, you were able to turn around before you fell into that dark hole." "Yes mam, I was struggling with my own pain, and trying to figure out how I could help you with yours. There were days when I just didn't know what to do or where to turn. You had convinced me that God was not hearing your prayers, so I believed that he wouldn't hear mine either." "I am so sorry baby, please forgive me." "There's nothing to forgive mommy, I love you so." "Yes, there is something to forgive," said Damon. I worried myself to the bones about the two of you and defended you guys to grandma every time she had something to say about the two of you. I was tired and felt as if I was carrying your burdens on my shoulders." "I'm sorry Damon, will you please forgive me," asked Jackie. "Me too Damon, I'm sorry, will you forgive me too?" Damon looked at his mom and sister with a smirky look on his face, then burst into laughter. "I am just messing with you guys; I love you more than pizza and there's nothing I wouldn't do for you. You don't have to apologize to me ever, for leaning on me. I am just glad that these little bones of mine were strong enough to hold you up." "Yes, they were said Jackie as she reached over and embraced her son.

When Grace finally woke up from the chair, it was after midnight. She looked around to see if Jackie and the children were still there. There was no sign of them, so she called out to them. "Jackie, Zelia, Damon, are you guys still here?" When she didn't receive a response, she looked at her watch to check the time. "Oh goodness, no wonder no one answered, I must have slept through their noises." She stood up and stretched her arms up as high as they would reach. "Tard, I think they got it; they finally got it." With tears in her eyes, she walked into her bedroom, took a pillow from the bed, and threw it on the floor. She knelt on the pillow beside the bed and began to pray. She gave God thanks for allowing them time to get it together. She praised him for all the blessings he had given to them; and she asked him for his continued blessings and for his mercy. She stayed on her knees so long that she had to ask Jesus to help her up.

When she had gotten up from kneeling, she got herself ready for bed. When she laid down, she began to remanence about her past life. She remembered many mountains she'd climbed, and the hills she had to cross, and all the obstacles that were thrown in her way, but what she remembered the most, was how God brought her over those mountains, and across those hills, and how he guided her around those obstacles, and how he sustained her, loved her, and forgave her. She was so thankful for her life, because each chapter, no matter how good or bad, was a lesson learned. The lessons she learned were tools for her survival and strengthened her for her mission of showing others where to turn in good times, and in bad. She never saw herself as a perfect woman, but she loved perfectly, and that was about as close as she thought she would get to perfection. This time when she closed her eyes, it was morning, and the sun was shining bright before she reopened them.

Grace was pleased with the way her day had gone yesterday. She hopped out of bed and headed for the bathroom. She wanted to be prepared for whatever came her way today. She was so excited that she forgot to give God thanks for keeping her through the night and waking her up. She stopped in her spot, raised her hands, and gave God praise and thanks, and asked for his continued blessings. After she'd showered and prepared for the day, she went into the kitchen to make breakfast. Grace had retired a few years back, so she didn't have to go to work. She was, however, involved in several community projects, that kept her on the go. She loved serving the community and had reconnected herself to them as well when she reconnected to the church. She took her time starting her morning. She knew that Jackie would still be asleep, and that the children would be in school. After she finished her breakfast, she went out on the porch to take in some sun and fresh air. As she sat swinging on her porch swing, she decided to plan out her agenda for the day.

The first thing Grace had on her agenda was to check on some of the sick and close in, in her neighborhood. From there, she planned to go by the nursing home and volunteer for a few hours. She still wasn't feeling her best, but she was determined to push herself through. After she had completed planning out her day, she stood up from sitting on her swing, and went back inside. When she entered the kitchen, her phone began ringing in her skirt pocket. She took it out to see who was calling her and was shocked to see Jackie's name showing in the call ID. "Hello Jackie." "Hi mom, how are you doing this morning?" "I am fine but a little surprise that you are up and calling me so early in the morning." "Oh, I've been up for hours." Hours: Is everything alright, are the children, ok?" "Yes mom, everything's just fine." "Then why so early, did you have a problem sleeping?" "Somewhat; last night after the children and I left your house I felt the need to pray, so after the children had gone into their rooms, I got down on my knees and made a long prayer to God. When I got up, I felt different, like God had truly heard my prayer. Then, I decided to have a conversation with him." "That must have been interesting." "Yes, it was, because for the first time in my life I was able to hear his voice. He spoke to me and told me that I am healed by his stripes. He told me to take up my cross and follow him. He said he had been waiting for me. I was so excited that I jumped out of bed and made breakfast for the kids before they left for school. Damon and Zelia were surprised to see me in the kitchen and for the first time in a long while, didn't have to eat cold cereal for breakfast." "Sounds to me you had quite a night." "I did mom, and to add to that I am going back to work. I realize that there's a whole lot of people far worse off than I am and they are making the best of their situations and their lives. I am no longer going to sit in my pity and use my condition as an excuse to fail."

Grace was so astonished that she could barely speak. If Jackie could see her through the phone, she would have seen streams of tears rolling from her mother's eyes. When she was finally able to get out a word, she said in a soft voice, "Jackie, this is the day I have been praying for, for so long. So, tell me, what's next?" "Well, Zelia asked before she left for school this morning if we could come over this evening or tonight and finish listening to your stories. She also said that she has some questions that she would like to ask you." "If it's alright with you, may we come over around six this evening?" "Sure, I will be finished with all my chores by then and you guys can finish off that left over from yesterday." "Sounds like a plan mom, we will see you later today."

When Grace hung the phone up from Jackie, her eyes were still filled with tears, but they were tears of joy and happiness. She was so happy that she wanted to shout. She began singing and praising God for what he had just done for her child. Her prayers for Jackie had been answered. She had never given up on Jackie, or lost faith that she would one day find her way back, even though sometimes she did get wary. As she pranced around the kitchen singing and praising God, she thought of Tard; he would be so proud of his little girl.

Grace was always happy when she knew that Jackie and her grandkids were coming for a visit, but today, she was beside herself with excitement. The children visited their grandmother regularly, but Jackie seldom came with them. When Jackie and the children arrived, Grace greeted each of them with hugs and kisses; one might have thought that she had not seen them in years. She went into the kitchen where she had taken out the leftovers and heated them up before they arrived. "Come on inside and get yourselves comfortable, said Grace. It is so good to see you again so soon Jackie." Jackie understood all too well what her mother was referring to, so she smiled and took it all in stride. The old Jackie would have had a snappy comeback for her mom.

Dinner was over and the kitchen was cleaned once again. Everyone was stuffed and stretched out on a chair. "So Zelia" asked Grace, I hear you have some questions for me." Zelia sat upright on her chair, and looking directly into her grandmother's eyes, said yes grandma, I do." "What type of questions, what do you need to know?" Remember last night when I told you I understood what you were saying about purpose and beauty?" "Yes, I do. You seemed to have grasp the concept very well, especially for someone your age." "Yes, and I did; I even gave examples of my friend's mother and her situations, and you gave examples of your purpose, and your beauty, and mom's purpose and her beauty, but what about me grandma?" I know you said that we must find our own purpose, and I've been searching, but I need help. Can you point me in the direction of my purpose, and the beauty at the end of my suffering?" Grace was amazed by her granddaughter's wisdom. "Yes Zelia, I can point you in the direction, but the revelation has to be yours." "Okay grandma, then start pointing." Grace was always amused by Damon and Zelia's sense of humor and began laughing as she said, "Zelia my dear, you are a riot."

Grace folded her arms across her chest and began speaking. "Zelia, you asked your purpose for the pain and suffering you are going through. And you want to know where the beauty lies within or at the end of it." "Yes grandma, that sums it up." "Have you ever stopped to think that the purpose of your pain was to give purpose to your mother, and the beauty, is her ability to once again be the type of mother that the two of you deserve. It is also a beautiful thing that your mom has regained her faith and trust in God. It wasn't me that did it, it was you. When you as a child were willing to listen, it made your mom listen as well. One can never hear if they do not listen. Now that I have pointed you in the right direction, I pray that you are able to figure out the rest. Seek God's face and ask him to direct you." "Thanks grandma, you have done it again. You certainly are a wise old owl." "I am only as wise as God allows me to be. He speaks, and I listens."

After Grace had answered all Zelia's questions, she seemed to be satisfied with the answers. "Ok grandma, I know that I sidetracked you, but can you finish telling us the rest of the stories now?" "Grace looked over at Jackie and asked, "is it okay, don't they have homework?" "It's okay mom, the teachers have a workday tomorrow, so they don't have school. They can stay up for a while longer." Damon who had been quiet during the entire evening, sat up on his chair and said, I have heard enough about pain to last me a lifetime, can't we please change the subject, and can we watch a movie on the tv?" Everyone burst into laughter. Damon looked at them as if they had fallen from a turnip truck, he didn't see anything funny. "Ok Damon," said Grace, I realize that discussing pain does not affect you directly, at least not now, but if you live awhile, you will know exactly why we are having these discussions. Everyone experience pain at some point in their lives, some more than others; being armored to handle it means that you are ahead of the situation." "Why, why do we have to suffer pain?" "Because it makes us stronger, makes us humble, remember when I told you to read **1 Peter** chapter ten and verse twelve?" let me refresh you; "And after you have suffered a little while, the God of all grace, who has called you to his eternal glory in Christ, will himself restore, confirm, strengthen, and establish you." "So, what you are saying is that we all have to suffer?" "It is not so much that you have to suffer, the suffering is a test, the purpose is your lesson, and the beauty is your reward." "When we suffer, we look for the outcome, and only we can determine how we will end. Will we go through quietly, will we be loud, will we complain, of will we be humble, will we rejoice and put our trust in God?" Those are all options along with some others." "Like what grandma, what are some of the other options?" "Some people choose to end their lives, some choose to indulge in alcohol or other drugs, some give up, and so the list goes on." "Oh my, the switch just came on in my head. I can really see where you are going with this. It's like reading a good book. You know that it's good, but you don't know how it is going to end." "Well, that is a different way of looking at it, but if that's the way you understand it, that's good." "Okay grandma, I'm in, said Damon, tell us the rest of the story." "Gladly, said Grace, as soon as you bring me a glass of water, my throat is dry." Damon hurried to the kitchen and returned with a sparkling glass of water for his grandmother. "Thank you, Damon, now let me see how I will begin.

"Remember when I told you that there is purpose and beauty when it comes to pain?" "Yes," said Zelia, "I remember." "Remember how I gave examples so that it would help you understand?" "Yes, we do," responded Jackie. "Well, I am going to give you the perfect example that you will have no trouble understanding. It will open your eyes to everything I said leading up to this point." "Tell me grandma, I can't wait to hear it," said Zelia. "Actually, you have heard it told many times, but as human's sometimes do, we take things for granted, or we get excited when we first hear it, then we have the tendency to compartmentalize it." "So, if we already know it, why are you telling us again grandma?" asked Damon. "Yes, you've heard it before, but you tell me, after I explain it to you from another perspective, if you don't see it differently, yet the same." "That sounds complicated grandma," said Damon. "Life often is complicated, but the strong will figure it out, and will survive. We have only two eyes, but many ways of looking at things. How you look at a situation will determine how you approach it, and how you approach it will determine how you cope with the outcome." "Now if you will be quiet for just a few minutes, I will explain it all to you."

Jackie, Zelia, and Damon sat quietly on the chair in anticipation of what Grace was about to share with them. "Okay grandma, said Zelia, we are all ears." "Sounds to me, that some of us are all mouths, laughed Grace, but alright, let me hit the reset button." Grace was sitting across the room from the others in her comfortable rocking chair, but not so far that they couldn't hear her loud and clear. She cleared her throat and began her story.

"Damon, you asked, "why we have to suffer so much pain." "Well, if you go back to the book of Genius, and read it again you will understand why. Just as the serpents must crawl on their bellies and eat dust the rest of their lives, so does man have to bear pain. I am not going to tell you the story of Adam and Eve again because you have heard it many times, but what I will tell you is that because of our disobedience, we are all prone to pain, no exemptions." Before eating the forbidden fruit, Adam didn't have to labor, and Eve didn't have to bear the pain of childbearing." "You remember how the snake convinced Eve to eat the forbidden fruit in the garden of Eden and how Eve convinced Adam to eat of the same fruit don't you?" "Yes mam, I sure do, if Adam wasn't so weak, we wouldn't have to work so hard," said Damon. "If Adam had not eaten from the tree of knowledge, there would be no you," said Grace. "Before eating the fruit from the forbidden tree, Adam and Eve had no knowledge that they were naked, or that they were different, if you know what I mean." "Do you mean that if they had not eaten from the tree of good and evil, they would never have known to be together as man and wife grandma?" asked Zelia. "That is exactly what I'm saying Zelia, but it was all in God's plan." "You see, after they ate from the tree that they were told not too, God cursed them. He told Eve that she would multiply her sorrow and her conception: he said that in sorrow she would bring forth children, and that her husband would rule over her. Go ahead, read it again, **Genisis 3:16**, and then **Genesis 3:17-3:19** where he told Adam that because he chose to listen to Eve and ate from the tree instead of obeying his command, "cursed is the ground for thy sake: in sorrow thou shall eat of it all the days of thy life; thorns and thistles shall it bring forth to thee; and thou shall eat the herb of the field." By the sweat of your brow, you will eat your food until you return to the ground, since from it you were taken; for dust you are and to dust you will return." "So, you see, there's no way to avoid pain, but we should strive to manage them." "So, grandma, are you saying that everyone has to suffer pain?" "Yes, that is what I am saying, at some point in life, we all will feel the sting of some type of pain." "The story of Adam and Eve tells us the origin of pain, but the example that I promised you above all examples is about the one call Jesus." Grace had captured everyone's attention, even Jackie's who had been nodding off.

"Jesus suffered unimaginable pain when he walked the earth in the flesh. He suffered physical torment, emotional trauma, and spiritual agony. He was tortured and beaten with multiple leather cords twisted together, while his hands were tied to a tree, by the roman soldiers as a crowd of spectators looked on. After he was whipped, he was dragged away by the soldiers to the governor's palace where they rammed a crown made of thorns down on his head. While the blood was running down Jesus's face, they began hitting him on his head with an object that drove the thorns deeper into his head. After cramming the thorns into his head, they took away his robe and led him outside the city to be crucified. Jesus was beaten beyond recognition and was forced to carry the heavy cross through the street. Because of his brutal beating, Jesus was weak, and he stumbled and collapsed. A stranger by the name of Simon reached down and picked up the cross and took it the rest of the way, to the top of the hill. When they reached the top of the hill, they threw Jesus to the ground on the same back that they had beaten the blood out of. Then they took Jesus's hands and places iron stakes around his wrist and drove nails into them. They also nailed his feet to the cross." Just imagine how painful this must have been, I can't begin to imagine. While Jesus hung there on that cross, he was rejected, insulted, falsely accuse, and spat on. They even divided up his clothes and cast lots for them." Jesus, who had done no wrong, was hanging there on a tree, bleeding, suffering, and calling out to his God. When the time came, he gave up the ghost and died."

When Grace had finished telling them of the pain and sufferings of Jesus, they were all in tears. "Mom said Jackie; I have read and heard that story told more times than I can remember, but this is the first time I was able to identify. This was the first time that I saw Jesus as a human being. Before, I saw him as a story in a book, but what I don't quite understand is what beauty came from his suffering?" The way he was demeaned, demoralized, and discounted, how is that beautiful?" Remember Jackie, I never said that pain was beautiful, I said that beauty comes as a result of pain. Now maybe some might phrase it differently than I have. Some might say that "beauty is the result of pain," or "no pain no gain," or "there's a civil lining," or "that there's a rainbow at the end of every storm," "that weeping may endure for a night but joy cometh in the morning," or "the "darkest part of night is just before dawn;" or there's a promise land at the end of the wilderness;' or there's sunshine after the rain;' or that there's a trophy at the end of the race;'" or may be even that there are streets of gold, and pearly gates, and angel wings;" but no matter what the phrase, the end result is still the same, if you trust and believe." Ok, momma, I understand." "Do you, do you really?" Let me paraphrase just a little Jackie."

There was our Jesus, thorns pressed down on his head until he bled, nails in his hands and feet as he hung on a cross; demeaned, demoralized, criticized, lied on, spat on and crucified: Oh, what pain! But he had a purpose! After all his suffering, crucifixion, and burial, he rose, with all power in those same nailed printed hands. What mighty hands! Because of his pain and suffering we all have the beauty of salvation! Now just look at the beauty that came from his suffering! Imagine that! Can you see the beauty, can you feel the beauty, can't you feel the love that our God has laid upon us. The blessing of Jesus Christ. He loves us so that he sent his only son down here in this hate filled world to suffer and die for us. But not only did he suffered and died for us, but he rose for us, and he lives for us. Now it doesn't get any more beautiful than that."

"What about those people that get sick and never get better. What beauty is there for them, and what was the purpose of their pains?" asked Zelia. "That is a million-dollar question Zelia," responded Grace. "We cannot say that those people died from their pain, or that they did not understand their purpose. Each person must recognize their own purpose and appreciate their own beauty. My recognition of your purpose serves no purpose, unless you are able to recognize and accept it. Every individual is different in their circumstances, so their needs may be different, their objective may be different, even their approach may be different. Trying to figure out someone else's purpose is exhausting and sometimes evasive. Especially if you are uncertain about your own life's purpose and direction. What I can say though, is that the beauty of heaven awaits us, if we have prepared ourselves.

What about the people that's going to hell momma, where are their beauty?" asked Jackie. They were given the same gifts as us, but they chose not to unwrap them, so they receive momentary beauty, but those of us that believe, will receive everlasting beauty, the beauty of heaven. I don't know about you, but all the beauty that I received on earth does not begin to compare to the beauty of heaven." Damon, who was mostly quiet during the entire conversation, decided to speak up. "So, grandma, this beauty that you are speaking of, are we going to have to wait until we get to heaven to receive it." "Are you in heaven now?" "No mam." "Is your mother in heaven?" "No mam." "What about me Damon, am I in heaven?" "No grandma, why are you asking me if you guys are in heaven?" "Because it seems that you have missed out on some of what I said." Zelia felt the need to answer

Damon's question; "Damon, no, we do not have to wait to get to heave to receive the beauty that comes after pain or painful experiences, just look around, mom and grandma went through great pain giving birth to us, but look at me, see how beautiful I am." "That's a good example Zelia, but I'm not just talking about your physical appearance, though you are beautiful, I am referring to the beauty of the experience, and how the pain has been forgotten." If you study your Bible, you will find that God does not look at our external beauty, but he looks at our internal beauty, such as how we love, our kindness and endurance for others, our contentment, our ability to forgive, our self-control, and our meekness and humility." "But to answer your question Damon, Jesus left us the beautiful gift of the Holy Spirit. It is free to all that wants it." "Why wouldn't someone want it?" "Why wouldn't someone want Jesus? When you answer that you will be a miracle worker." "Oh, I know the answer to that one," said Zelia. "Do tell," said

Jackie. "The reason some people don't want Jesus is because they prefer the devil." "You are absolutely right baby, now the reason that is, I don't know, but you are so right."

When Grace had told her story and answered all the questions her daughter and grandchildren had, it was getting late in the night. "Grandma, since we don't have school tomorrow, can we just spend the night here with you," asked Zelia. "That is fine with me, if it's ok with your mom." "Yes mama, it's ok; we will all stay the night." Grace was happy that Jackie and the children were spending the night, it seemed like old times. She looked over at her daughter with a heart filled with love and said, "Now, you see what beauty we've found here tonight. All that hell you put me through, and all those sleepless nights wondering where you were and if you were alright, and now look; you are here with me and the children, spending the night, with renewed faith, and purpose driven; oh, what a **BEAUTFUL SIGHT!**"


**Isaiah 33:17**: "Your eyes will behold the king in his beauty; they will see a land that stretches afar."

Barbara Williams Brown

www.ingramcontent.com/pod-product-compliance
Lightning Source LLC
Chambersburg PA
CBHW021112080526
44587CB00010B/492